A
UM
HOCKEY

My thanks to all who have so willingly contributed to this, the third
edition of *A Guide to Umpiring Hockey* – their enthusiasm for the
project has been my motivation.

I make special mention of the many umpires, players and coaches
who have so willingly offered their time and input, VJ Design, (design
and artwork), and all who feature in photographs – thank you.

Jane Nockolds
World Panel Hockey Umpire

Published by: Sports Resources Ltd., 39 High Street South, Stewkley, Bucks LU7 0HP, UK
                   T/F: +44 (0) 1525 240128
                   E: info@sportsresources.co.uk
                   www.sportsresources.co.uk

Date published: September 2003
ISBN: 0-9541169-2-5
Designed by: VJ Design (E: info@vjdesign.co.uk)
Photographs by: Paul Coleshill, Jane Hodgson

CONTENTS

INTRODUCTION

Jane Nockolds coaching a young umpire

The Rules of hockey have changed considerably in recent years and the speed and skills of the game have increased immensely. Consequently, few people would argue that umpiring and umpires must continue to make every effort to move forward with the game.

Key to good umpiring performance is keeping up to speed with the game and there are a number of components that are key to the process. These include a thorough knowledge of the Rules, the ability to read the game, a willingness to listen and speak with coaches, players and other umpires, and most important of all, a desire to seek continual improvement.

The purpose of this book is to help you in your efforts to achieve a higher level of performance, thereby increasing your enjoyment and confidence. It aims to better equip you to deal with situations common to the game as they occur. Throughout are useful tips, guidance and thought provoking advice from a number of umpires of all levels including internationals from around the world – and please don't suppose that the advice is specific only to international hockey... all of us benefit from the experience of others and the tips I have selected are pertinent to all levels of the game.

I do hope that you will enjoy and benefit from this, the third edition of *A Guide to Umpiring Hockey.*

Jane Nockolds

World Panel Hockey Umpire

Please note: For the purpose of simplicity all gender references are written as he/him.

INTRODUCTION

3

Chapter 1

PREPARING TO UMPIRE

Very few of us are able to umpire well at our first attempt, so here are six suggestions to help you before you go out to umpire your first match.

1 Read about umpiring.

If you are or were a player, you will have an understanding of the Rules of hockey and be able to recognise the reason for a penalty.

As an umpire, you need to think about the application of the Rules and understand them not as pages in a book, but as what is actually happening in front of you – on the pitch.

2 Watch a match.

Don't go just to see the play. Watch the umpires and see how they apply the Rules and control the match.

- Notice that the two umpires meet before the match. During this time they discuss principles and make decisions including essentially how they will operate as a team and, as individuals in terms of responsibility and control. The umpires arrange and confirm cooperation techniques and how to effectively communicate throughout the match.
- They check that the pitch is correctly marked, that the goal posts are placed immediately behind the back-lines and that the nets are firmly attached to the posts and the cross-bar, so there can be no doubt when the ball has entered the goal. They also decide who shall time

each half and which side of the pitch they will take. The normal playing time is seventy minutes, each half being thirty-five minutes in length.

....

- It is advisable that umpires carry a supply of string or adhesive tape (insulating tape is perfect for the job) and a penknife or a pair of scissors so that they can repair or secure damaged or loose-fitting nets before the match begins. Although this responsibility primarily rests with the home team, evidence suggests that they rarely have the equipment to deal with it. Do them a favour and be equipped to handle it!

....

- When the match begins – watch the umpire on your side of the pitch. Notice how he moves almost continually, with the play, especially when the ball is in or approaching his half of the pitch. Notice the positioning of the umpire in relation to play.
- See where the umpire stands for set-pieces. These include free-hits, hit-ins, penalty corners, corners and penalty strokes.
- Notice the umpire's signals. They should always be clear and given with confidence.

Initially you may only recognise some of the offences. You will certainly not see everything, but gradually the picture will become clearer and you will recognise more and apply the penalties appropriately when you start umpiring.

A Guide to – UMPIRING HOCKEY
PREPARING TO UMPIRE

3 Two things you can practice at any time:

- **Signalling.** Silly as it may seem, this is best practised in front of a mirror. You may find that what you believe you are doing is not what you see in your mirror, and that is exactly what the players would see. Could they be confused by your signals? Do you look suitably confident? Try to get your signals right before you go out to umpire. They really are important.
- **Blowing the whistle.** Experiment with your technique. It is important to be able to speak with your whistle. You need to learn to vary the tone. When a serious offence occurs, you will need to blow the whistle strongly. This is often referred to as a blast. When a minor offence occurs, a quieter whistle is preferred...just a beep to stop the play and award the penalty.

....

- Remember that you must appear to be confident.
Sometimes a slow or hesitant signal, or a spluttery
whistle is considered proof of uncertainty. Try to avoid it.

....

4 **Umpiring Clothing.**

Most hockey teams have an attractive team kit. They look smart and distinctive. Umpires also should look smart and have distinctive kit. It is important that the players can quickly distinguish the umpires. They don't want or have time to search for you or loose sight of you. You must avoid merging into the spectators in the background or other players on the pitch. Umpires should wear shirts of the same colour, dark coloured (ideally black) trousers or skirts and footwear selected according to the playing surface.

5 Equipment.

The equipment you need includes a copy of the current Hockey Rules book, two whistles (one a spare), a stop-watch (preferably worn on your wrist as opposed to around your neck), a set of coloured warning cards, a pen or pencil, and a notepad, (or match score card), for recording the score and the number of a player or players receiving an official warning (ie a card or cards).

6 Get to know umpires.

Someone in your club who is interested in your progress will be able to help you. In addition, every area or region has an umpiring secretary or administrator and a number of umpire coaches. There are regular events for umpires in most areas. These include lectures, presentations and coaching days and evenings. The benefits of attending these events go beyond extending your umpiring knowledge and skills – you find yourself among new friends and new opportunities become available to you.

Preparing to umpire involves all of the following:
- Reading, learning and understanding the Rules of Hockey.
- Regularly watching experienced umpires.
- Practising blowing a whistle and signalling.
- Talking with coaches and players.
- Taking every opportunity to meet other umpires.
- Attending lectures, presentations and umpire coaching events.

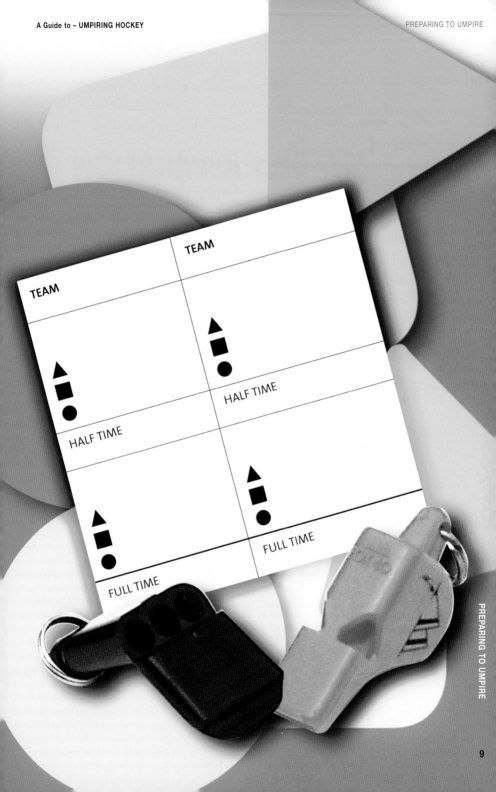

Chapter 2

MATCH PREPARATION

Umpires should make every effort to be at the venue at least thirty minutes before the match is due to start. After their pre-match chat (see below) they should quickly check the pitch markings, the goals and the flags and make sure that the nets are in good order. Then it's time to whistle up the Captains to toss a coin and decide which team will take the ball (the centre pass) – the other team will choose ends (which end of the pitch to attack or defend). The winner of the toss has first choice.

....

- Try to get the toss underway promptly. If it's possible, aim for 15 minutes before the start time. Too often, umpires call the captains to toss the coin with only seconds remaining...the captain is busy briefing the team, or the team are going through the last 'crucial' penalty corner drills... bad timing umpire...not the best start to your game!

....

Things to discuss in the pre-match chat:
- You are the "third team" on the pitch – how will you work **together?**
- How will you be consistent and fair?
- How will you communicate and help each other and the players?
- What happens if it all goes horribly wrong? (You can't run away!)

- What about advantage?
- What about raised ball?
- What about applying the 5m Rule?
- Who will bring time back in, (signal readiness for the re-start), when it has been stopped because of injury or incident?
- How about eye-contact... particularly in and around the circles? This is key to the process of you working together effectively. It is essential to your game plan – your management and your control.

In addition, there are more trivial things to discuss, such as who will take which side of the pitch and who will time the first half etc.

So, as you can see, the importance of arriving at the venue at least 30 minutes before the game is due to start is very genuine. If you seriously want to perform well and be of benefit to the match, you must get there early and spend quality time discussing and planning with your colleague.

Chapter 3

STARTING AND RE-STARTING THE MATCH

The Centre Pass

The match is started, re-started after half-time, and after each goal is scored, by a pass taken from the centre of the pitch. It is called the centre pass and it may be made in **any direction.** It can go forwards, backwards or sideways, however, it should not be intentionally lifted. (See chapter 9, Raised Ball).

The pass at the start of the match is taken by the team who did not choose (at the toss) which end of the pitch to attack or defend. The opposing team takes the pass at the start of the second half. Following a goal being scored or awarded, the match is restarted by the team who conceded the goal.

Reminders for the umpire:

1 The ball must be stationary and in the centre of the pitch.
2 All players (other than the taker) must be in their own half and all opposition players must be **at least 5m from the ball** until the pass is taken.
3 The pass may be directed in **any direction** – backwards, forwards or sideways.
4 The taker must not play the ball again or approach within playing distance **until it has been touched by another player of either team.**
5 The ball cannot be played by another player of the same team before it has moved at least **one metre.**

And where are you the umpire while all of this is happening?

The best place is reasonably into the pitch. About 10 to 12m is good. Be close enough to see everything and be alert to the movements of the players. Do your best to stay clear of the ball and the play, but remember always that you are not a mere spectator...get into the game, and move with the game.

....

- Don't be tempted to get too close but neither is there any need for you to 'glue' yourself to the side line.

....

Good positioning of the umpire in relation to play

Chapter 4

THE BULLY

The bully appears to have been a part of hockey forever, and when you talk about the game to people who don't follow hockey closely, it is always the bully that they remember!

As the Rules currently stand, the game can be re-started with a bully for any one of three reasons:

1 Following a simultaneous offence by players of opposing teams.
2 Following an accident or incident from which there was no offence.
3 If the ball has to be replaced.

It is important to remember that the bully cannot be taken within 14.63m of the back-line, (the radius of the shooting circle).

....

• The players are often unfamiliar with this Rule, so if there is an incident requiring a bully and it's within 14.63m of the back-line, step in promptly, remove the confusion and advise where it is to be taken, (in line with the incident 14.63m from the defending back-line).

....

Reminders for the umpire:

• The ball must be stationary and in the correct place.
• The players taking the bully must face each other with their own back-line to their right. They must remain square to each other until their sticks have touched (ie touched the ground and then touched sticks).

....

- The fundamental characteristics of the Bully have been retained for many years, but now (commencing 1st January 2004) the Rule has been simplified by requiring sticks to touch only **once.**

....

More reminders for the umpire:

- The flat surface of the sticks must touch above the ball.
- Until the bully has been completed, all other players must remain a minimum of **5m** from the ball.

The signal for a Bully

....

- If the takers don't comply with these conditions the bully must be retaken. However, if a player infringes the bully more than once, you should award a free-hit to the opposing team.

....

Chapter 5

METHODS OF SCORING

A goal is scored when the ball passes completely over the goal-line between the posts and under the crossbar – the ball having been played by, or off, an attacking player from within the circle. The only exception is a penalty goal and that is governed by the Penalty Stroke Rule. We will look at that later in the book. (See Chapter 7, Penalties).

Reminders for the umpire:

- A ball on the goal-line is not in the goal. The whole ball must cross the goal-line before a goal can be scored.

....

- Very unusual, but should the ball break and only part of it enter the goal, no goal is scored. If you see the ball break, you should blow the whistle immediately, stop time and request a replacement ball. Re-start the play with a bully... and remember, no bully within 14.63m of the back-line.

....

- The circle line (edge) is part of the circle, therefore a goal can be scored if the ball is played on the line by an attacker, even though the player may be outside the circle.

- The attacker need not be the last person to touch or play the ball for a goal to be scored. Providing the ball was in the circle when the attacker touched or played it, it makes no difference if it is touched by a defender before it enters the goal.

Therefore, unless the ball has been touched in the circle by an attacker, no goal can be scored. If the ball is played outside the circle and then is deflected into the goal by a defender, your decision, (the correct decision), is to award a **corner** which can be taken from either side of the pitch.

- Signal for the corner quickly then you will prevent any unnecessary confusion. A surprising number of players think it is a goal if the ball has been touched by **any** player in the circle!

Chapter 6

WHEN THE BALL GOES OUT OF PLAY

Hit-out (14.63m hit)

Let's keep this easy. The hit-out should be awarded to the defence when an **attacker** has played the ball over the back-line and no goal is scored – that is, it was wide of or over the goal-posts, or between the goal-posts from a hit or deflection which was outside the circle.

Before the hit-out is taken, the umpire should check that:

- The ball is opposite where it went over the back-line and not more than 14.63 m from the back-line. (Don't be fussy...an extra few centimetres are of little consequence.)
- All opposition players are at least 5m from the ball.
- When the ball is played, it must move at least one metre before it is played by a member of the same team.

....

- It is a good idea to show the 5m signal or say "5m please", before the hit is taken or alternatively give the whistle one little beep to remind the players to retreat a little more.

The signal for the hit-out

- Don't be pedantic and intrusive – Avoid being thought of as someone who interrupts the game only because an opponent isn't quite 5m from the ball as the hit is taken. Quickly consider what influence or disadvantage was caused...perhaps his lack of distance was of no relevance to the play and blowing the whistle would be unnecessary.

- If the ball rises off the ground, penalise it **only** if it is dangerous or threatening to a player or players.

....

Hit-In from the side-line

If a player plays or deflects the ball completely over the side-line, you should award a hit-in to the opposing team. Before the hit-in is taken, check that all opposition players are at least 5m from the ball.

....

- Don't be excessively fussy. Sometimes the players want to do things very quickly and the ball may be a few centimetres off the line when they place it for the hit...let it go without interfering.

- If an opposition player is too close, the umpire may want to quickly blow the whistle a second time and indicate that the player withdraw to the necessary

The signal for the hit-in

distance. Alternatively the **best** way to send the
message effectively is to be close and to show a big
5 – a hand with all fingers splayed...

....

Reminders for the umpire when awarding a hit-in:

1 The ball is on the side-line, close to the point where it went over the side-line. The taker may stand on or off the pitch.

2 The ball should be hit or pushed, not scooped or flicked. Remember there is no need to penalise the taker if the ball lifts off the pitch, unless it was **intentionally** lifted and/or **dangerous.**

3 The ball must move at least one metre before it can be played by another player of the same team.

4 The taker must not approach or play the ball again, before it has been touched by another player.

Following any breach of the Rule, you should award a free-hit to the opposition.

....

• Remember that a ball **on** the side-line is on the
pitch. Most of the time the players want to take the hit-
in quickly. Allow them to do so.

• When a hit-in is awarded or a free-hit is close to
the near edge of the pitch, adopt a wide
position (ideally off the pitch) to maximise your arc of

vision. In addition, make sure that your decision has credibility by being close. The **closer you are, the more weight your decision carries** and occasionally players from both teams claim that the hit-in should be theirs!

• When the hit-in is at your end of the pitch you really need to be within 10m of it. When it is at the very far end of the pitch, (down near the corner), try to be **approximately 10**m over the centre line. After all, 45m is a long way, (half the length of the pitch), and if you are called upon to make a decision, you will need to see everything clearly and your decision must have credibility.

....

Chapter 7

PENALTIES

Free-Hit

When a free-hit is awarded, it should be taken close to where the incident occurred; the ball should be stationary and when played, it must move at least one metre before it can be played by a member of the same team.

....

- Be aware of the purpose of awarding the free-hit...it is to restore ball possession to the deserving team. Know that the players often want to take the free hit quickly. You should be looking to see that the opposition retreat quickly so as to be at least 5m from the ball. However, remember that they need to be given fair time to retreat. You shouldn't penalise them if they are genuinely attempting to retreat quickly.

- If the opposing team make no visible effort to retreat to the required distance or they intentionally run over the ball, blow the whistle again and progress the free hit further up the pitch, (up to 10m), that is unless it is within the 23m area, in which case, if it is the defending side offending, you are within the Rules to upgrade the penalty and award a penalty corner.

....

A free-hit can be hit or pushed but not intentionally lifted. The intention must be to keep it on the surface, therefore it cannot be flicked or scooped. However, if it does lift off the surface, you shouldn't penalise it, unless it is dangerous, likely to lead to dangerous play, or it gives the team taking it a genuinely unfair advantage.

If the free-hit is awarded within 5m of the circle edge, **all players except the taker,** must be at least 5m from the ball.

....

• This offence is now much easier to recognise due to an increasing number of pitches being marked with the broken 5m line painted around the circle edge. This new pitch marking has genuinely helped the umpires and the players in and around the circle.

....

After taking the hit, the taker must not approach within playing distance of the ball until it has been touched or played by another player.

If the free-hit is awarded to the defence within 14.63m of their defending back-line, they can if they choose, move the ball up to a maximum of 14.63m from the back-line (level with the top of the circle), in line with where the incident occurred.

....

• Most of the time the players want to take the free-hit quickly, particularly when it is close to the circle. Umpires, this is not the time to take a rest! Be prepared, get yourself into the best position to see whatever may come next and get there quickly. It is really important

that you try to read the game at all times – particularly
in this crucial area of the pitch.

....

Corner

The umpire should award a corner when the ball is **unintentionally** played
over the back-line by a defending player. It makes no difference where
the defending player is positioned. He can be anywhere on the pitch.

....

- There is one important exception that you must
remember and that is when the attacking player plays
the ball in the circle and the ball subsequently deflects
off a defending players' stick into the goal (which is
also part of the back-line). It is a goal you award...not
a corner!

....

The corner markers are 5m from the corners of the pitch, on the side-
lines. Before the corner is taken, you should check that the opposition
players are at least 5m from the ball, and once it's taken, the ball must
move at least 1m before it can be played by a player of the same team.

The corner must be taken from the side the ball crossed the back-line
(ie near-side of the goal or far-side). However, if it crosses the back-line
in the middle (ie over the cross-bar of the goal), it may be taken from
either side. The attacking players choose the side...not the umpire.

- Occasionally it can be very difficult to see which team last touched the ball. A good example is when a defending player stretches in with a long stick just as an attacker shoots for goal. If you are unsure and your colleague can't help you, (perhaps he's too far away or unsighted due to players in front of him) consider the angle that the ball crossed the back-line. If it flew off at an obscure angle, then the laws of physics should help you determine who last touched it.

And finally, when taking the corner, just the same as with any free-hit situation, the taker must not **intentionally** lift the ball or raise it dangerously. Neither should he approach the ball or play it again before another player has touched it. If any of these circumstances occur, you should award a free hit to the opposing team (the defence).

- Don't be excessively pedantic, understand and appreciate the efforts of the players. If the ball lifts off the surface by mere centimetres it is irrelevant. You need to ask yourself quickly "is it dangerous or likely to lead to dangerous play?" If the answer is no, the correct decision is simple... you must **not** blow the whistle. Let the players play.

Penalty Corner

The Penalty Corner Rule is arguably the most complex of the Hockey Rules. There are many things to remember and potentially even more to see.

One small thing to remember is that unlike the Corner Rule, a choice is available. The penalty corner can be taken from either side of the goal and it is the attacking team's choice.

The Rules currently allow for the penalty corner to be taken anywhere between the penalty corner markers and the edge of the circle on the back-line. The markers are 10m from each goal-post on the back-line.

Before the penalty corner is taken, you need to ensure that everyone is correctly positioned. The goal-keeper and four defenders defend the goal and they can position themselves anywhere behind the back-line, on condition that they are a minimum of 5m from the ball. (There is a 5m marker on each side of the goal on the back-line.) The remaining players in the defending team should be on, or beyond, the centre-line.

The attacking players can position themselves anywhere on the pitch outside of the attacking circle. As with the defence, they also must be a minimum of 5m from the ball prior to it being played.

How about the umpire? Where do you position yourself? We specifically consider your positioning later in the book. (See Chapter 16, Positioning). Meanwhile, here is a check-list for you.

Check the following:

- The ball is between the penalty corner marker and the circle edge on the back-line.
- The taker has at least one foot off the pitch, (ie behind the back-line)
- There are five defenders, including the goalkeeper, behind the back-line.
- The defenders are at least 5m from the ball.
- The remaining players of the defending team are at, or close to, the centre line.
- The attackers are outside the circle-edge.

- While you are checking each of these things, it's useful to position yourself towards the middle of the circle in front of the goal and hold one arm up high from the shoulder. This signal advises the attacking team to wait until everyone is in position. It's also very important for the defenders as they don't want to break the line prematurely. As soon as everyone is ready, step back into your position and then lower your arm. Be warned...don't lower your arm until you are in position – lowering it indicates that the penalty corner can commence. And one further little tip...occasionally you don't have a lot of time. You should avoid being seen to hold up the play – the players when they are ready, don't then want to have to wait for you! So, do all of your checking as quickly as possible!

When should a penalty corner be awarded?

Pending advantage, there are four circumstances. They are as follows:

1 A defending player **intentionally** playing the ball over the defending back-line from anywhere on the pitch.

- Think hard about the intentions of the defender. You must be positive that he genuinely intended to put the ball over the back-line. Never assume or guess.

2 An **intentional** offence by a defending player in the defending 23m area.

- Again it is very important to consider the word "intentional." Hard or perhaps clumsy tackles are **not** intentional offences and should not be penalised as intentional offences. In these circumstances, a free-hit is the correct penalty.

3 An **intentional** offence by a defending player in the circle, which neither prevents a goal from being scored, or deprives an attacker of actual or likely possession of the ball.

- In order to recognise this offence, good positioning is essential. It is very important that you are able to immediately see what would or could have happened to the ball.

- Always think "I must see the ball at all times" and this will encourage and help you to position yourself as best you can.

4 An **unintentional** offence by a defending player in the circle.

- This is often an offence where you and the game will benefit if you hold your whistle – wait just that little bit longer – perhaps the advantage is there to be taken!

What are the responsibilities of the attacking players?

- The player taking the penalty corner must hit or push the ball. If the ball is **intentionally** lifted by the taker, or it's dangerous in any way, you should blow the whistle and award a free-hit to the defence.

- The ball must move at least 1m before it can be played by another player of the same team. If it doesn't move 1m and the taker attempts to approach or play the ball again, you should award a free-hit to the defence. The free-hit can be taken on any spot in line with the offence up to 14.63m from the back-line – level with the top of the circle.

- Any number of attacking players can be positioned around the circle edge but not the attacking goalkeeper. He has to remain in his own half of the pitch at all times, unless he is taking a penalty stroke.

No players (attackers or defenders) are permitted to enter the circle until the ball is played.

MANDATORY EXPERIMENTAL RULE:

The Penalty Corner Rule has been amended to read that no shot at goal shall be made until the ball has travelled outside the circle. This Experiment removes the previous requirement whereby the attacking team had to stop the ball before they were able to make a shot at goal – that is unless it travelled beyond 5m of the circle edge. So...in short, immediately the ball has passed completely outside of the circle, it can be passed or taken by the possessor back into the circle and he can shoot without first stopping it.

If the first shot at goal is a hit, the ball is not permitted to cross the goal line at above the height of the back boards (ie 460mm) unless it is deflected off another attackers or defenders stick en route.

PENALTIES

• Umpires, if the deflection makes the shot
dangerous to another field player (ie he has to dive out
of the way), you should blow the whistle immediately
and award a free hit to the other team.

What are the responsibilities of the defending players?
- The defenders mustn't cross the back-line or goal-line before the penalty corner is taken.
- The defending team players on the centre line shouldn't cross it before the penalty corner is taken.

• Don't worry yourself particularly with the defending
players at the centre line. You have enough to think
about and see in the circle. Your colleague, the other
umpire, is responsible for the supervision of the players
on the centre line. However, he isn't going to focus
exclusively on them! It's more important that he is
available to you... to assist and share the responsibility
of controlling the corner.

What if something happens and you, the controlling
umpire (the one who awarded the corner) doesn't see it?
This is why your colleague needs to be attentive. You
should look to him for advice and he should offer you a
signal. He won't blow the whistle, you will, and you'll
award the penalty. Thank him afterwards. A discreet
little thumbs up is always appreciated.

• Sometimes the defenders on the back-line cross too early (ie before the ball has been played), and the temptation is not to blow your whistle immediately. Try not to be tempted! The very first time they break the line early, you should blow your whistle, thereby giving a strong message to all of the players. Have the penalty corner re-taken and let the players know why it is being re-taken.

It's only if they seem to habitually break early that you could perhaps delay with your whistle – that is wait and see if the attack cleanly stop the ball and have a chance to shoot at goal. If the stop is not clean, blow the whistle and award the penalty corner again, but if it is perfect... wait... play the advantage, and don't forget to signal it!

It's also important that you note that repeated early breaking of the back-line can result in a penalty stroke being awarded. That's a very strong reason for doing your best to prevent it and re-awarding the PC while advising the defence accordingly. If you appear to ignore early breaking off the back-line and then suddenly award a penalty stroke against the players without sufficient warning, your credibility and rapport with the players will be severely threatened or damaged.

....

If a penalty corner is awarded immediately before half-time or full-time, the Rules require it to be completed.

The details of this Rule clearly indicate the circumstances that determine when a penalty corner is completed (see below). With centralised timing, (ie with a technical table), it is expected that players know the Rules and will not stop playing if time is indicated. This is consistent with the procedure adopted for indoor hockey. If there is no technical table, it is the umpires who are directly responsible for controlling the time and they will be able to take into account the prolongation of the game. In all instances the umpires, (usually the umpire controlling the penalty corner), is responsible for observing and indicating when the penalty corner has been completed.

So when is the penalty corner over?

From January 2004, the Rule has been simplified and standardised regarding the specification of how a penalty corner is completed. Completion for substitution purposes is now consistent with completion at the end of half time and full time and is as follows:

1 When a goal is scored.

2 When an attacker commits an offence.

3 When the ball travels more than 5m outside the circle.

4 When the ball travels outside of the circle for the second time.

5 When the ball is played over the back-line by an attacker or unintentionally by a defender (ie another PC is not awarded).

6 When a defender commits an offence and another PC is not awarded.

7 When a penalty stroke is awarded.

Penalty stroke

A penalty stroke can be awarded for any one of three reasons –

1 An **intentional** offence by a defending player in the circle to prevent a goal being scored or to deprive an attacker of actual or likely possession of the ball.

2 An **unintentional** offence by a defending player in the circle that prevents the probable scoring of a goal.

3 Persistent breaking of the back-line by defending players while defending penalty corners.

....

- When a penalty stroke is awarded, time is stopped immediately. You don't have to signal time stopped on this occasion, because the penalty stroke signal automatically indicates accordingly. But don't forget to stop your watch! Time is re-started when the whistle is blown to resume play at the end of the penalty stroke...and don't forget to start your watch!

....

Rather like the penalty corner situation, there are a number of things for the umpire to check following the award of a penalty stroke. **Here is a check-list:**

- All non-involved players must position themselves beyond the near 23m line and ideally not at, or close, to the centre of the line where they will be a potential distraction to the defending goalkeeper.
- The goalkeeper must stand on the goal-line and not move his feet (take a pace), **until** the ball is played.

- From January 2004, the Rule has been rationalised. If the question were "what if the goalkeeper leaves the goal-line or moves either foot before the ball is played and in so doing he prevents a goal being scored"? The answer is "you should award another PS". For any other offence by a goalkeeper that prevents a goal being scored, you should award a goal. This is called a penalty goal.

- The defending goalkeeper must continue to wear the protective helmet and carry the stick. Any other protective equipment may be removed, although it's highly unlikely that anyone would choose to reduce protection when defending a penalty stroke!
- The taker mustn't take the stroke until the umpire blows the whistle. The umpire will blow the whistle immediately he is confident that both players are ready (in position).

- What happens if the taker plays the stroke before the whistle is blown? The answer is you should award a **free-hit to the defence.**

- From January 2004, the Rule regarding the taker and the limitation regarding the number of steps he is permitted to take is removed and it's replaced by a more sensible specification. It will require the player taking the penalty stroke to be behind the ball and within

PENALTIES

playing distance of it. (Playing distance is interpreted as an outstretched arm and an outstretched stick.)
- The taker mustn't feint or dummy at playing the ball.
- The taker mustn't follow the stroke...re-bounds are not permitted!
- The ball can be pushed, flicked, or scooped and may raise to any height.

- In today's modern game of hockey, you will often see the taker at a penalty corner place their stick immediately behind the ball and propel the ball while maintaining stick contact with the ball (ie a drag action). This is totally within the Rules at a penalty corner but is **not** permitted at a penalty stroke.

Following the award of a penalty stroke, your colleague should come to your end of the pitch and stand astride the back-line, to the right of the goalkeeper and approximately 5-7m from the goal-post. The role of your colleague is to determine whether or not the entire ball crosses the goal-line. If you, as the controlling umpire are unsure, you need only look to your colleague and he should provide you with a signal confirming whether or not the ball has completely crossed the goal-line.

- Always discuss penalty strokes and your respective responsibilities in your pre-match chat. It is absolutely crucial that you are confident when conducting a penalty stroke.

If a goal is scored or awarded, (ie a penalty goal), the game is re-started at the centre line with a pass to the team who conceded it. If a goal isn't scored or awarded, the game is re-started with a free-hit to the defence up to 14.63m from the centre of the back-line.

....

- Before you re-start the match, always check to see that your colleague is back in position (nearer the other half of the pitch) and essentially, he is looking at you. It is very embarrassing and potentially problematical if you allow the game to begin while the other umpire is still trekking back!

Chapter 8

OBSTRUCTION

Contrary to popular belief, obstruction is not a difficult Rule to understand and neither is it difficult to recognise or apply. Putting it simply, to obstruct means to block or deny access, and in order for access to be denied, access has to be sought. In other words, if the opponent (the tackler), is not in a position to tackle, and attempting to tackle, how can an opportunity to tackle be denied? How can the tackler be obstructed? The opponent (the tackler) must therefore:

- be in a position to tackle,
- intend to tackle and,
- time the tackle precisely.

The timing is crucial because until the tackler is in a tackling position and demonstrates an intention to make the tackle, the player in possession of the ball is entitled to move off with the ball in any direction, however, he must not back in to the tackler.

....

- Remember that the player in possession of the ball is entitled to face in any direction while collecting the ball. They can face their own goal, their opponents goal, or either side-line and until an actual and properly positioned tackle is attempted and access is denied, (either by using the body or the stick), obstruction **cannot** apply. This principle applies in stationary and moving situations. It means quite simply, that the responsibility is on the tackler. Until the tackler comes into the equation, the possessor can do almost anything!

....

To prevent the tackler from tackling, the possessor has three options. They are either:

- to move off with the ball
- to pass the ball, or
- to shield the ball.

Shielding the ball with the body, leg or stick is totally legal until the tackler attempts the tackle. If the timing of the tackle is right, it is then that access is measured as being denied and it is then that obstruction takes place.

The signal for obstruction is to hold crossed forearms in front of the chest.

....

• There is to be a new umpiring signal for stick obstruction from January 2004. It will be to hold one arm out and downwards in front of the body half-way between vertical and horizontal, and touch the forearm with the other hand.

• Very rarely is it necessary to signal obstruction. The players recognise it – they will usually require only a directional signal from you.

....

Third party Obstruction

This is exactly what it suggests – obstruction involving a third party ie a player from the team in possession of the ball using their stick or body (99.9% of the time it's the body), to prevent the tackler from tackling.

....

• It's easy to spot and all the umpire needs to con-sider is the distance factor – we must be thinking play-ing distance if we are considering 3rd party obstruction. Beyond playing distance is not worth thinking about!

....

Chapter 9

RAISED BALL

Again, this is quite a simple Rule. Like obstruction, it is not difficult to recognise. There are really only two principles to consider now. There were three but from January 2004 the aerial ball restrictions will change (see next Chapter).

The 2 principles are:

1   A player may not intentionally raise the ball from a hit, except for a shot at goal, (unless it's the first shot at a penalty corner)...

2   A player may not raise the ball intentionally at another player.

....

•   In each principle the Rule consistently refers to the word 'intentional'. This does not mean that if the ball were unintentionally raised, no offence has occurred. If the raised ball is dangerous or likely to lead to dangerous play, it should be penalised. If it is neither, then the correct course of action is to leave it alone. Don't interfere unnecessarily umpires!

....

Chapter 10

AERIAL BALL

This is not to be confused with the raised ball. The term 'aerial ball' refers to a ball that is intentionally raised and travels high over a **long distance**.

It is a very skilful piece of play and is becoming increasingly evident in all areas of the game; defenders use it to get out of trouble and midfielders use it to set up the attack – to bypass the opposition by sailing the ball over the top of them.

Unfortunately the ball doesn't always fall into the intended space and on occasions, there are two or more players underneath it. It is here that we umpires often struggle to see who was there first, who was best positioned to receive the ball.

The player who was there first, who was best positioned to receive the ball, is entitled to play the ball without interference. The entitlement is 5m of space to collect and control the ball on the ground. So, if the ball is falling into an area already occupied by more than one player and neither appears willing to retreat the required 5m, you should blow the whistle and award a free-hit to the opposing team, (the team who didn't lift it), and it should be taken from the place where the actual or potential danger occurs. In this particular situation, it is during the flight of the ball, and the free-hit should be awarded from the spot where the ball was originally lifted – that is the take-off point.

- Don't wait for the ball to fall between the players.
Blow the whistle as it begins to descend.

- Good positioning is essential in order to make the
correct judgment. If it's down your own line, it's often
best to move out – increase the arc of vision and assess
it with angle!

- When considering the raised ball or the
aerial ball, assess the situation quickly. Was the ball
safe on it's upward path, not threatening or dangerous
to any player? Was the ball safe on it's downward path
and finally, was it safe at the point of collection?

From January 2004, the Rule regarding the long aerial ball that lands
in the circle is to change. It will be permitted to land directly in the circle
but must not be dangerous (as with any other raised ball).

AERIAL BALL

Chapter 11

ADVANTAGE

The term most commonly used for advantage is 'to hold the whistle'. It means to refrain from blowing as the offence occurs. It is very often much more advantageous to the team who were, or are, in possession of the ball if the umpire lets the play continue without interruption.

Umpires develop their understanding and the application of advantage as their experience increases.

....

- Don't be nervous; instead be brave and you will quickly learn to blow the whistle or hold the whistle. But remember, once blown the decision is made!

- The Tip above is very clear. If you don't blow the whistle and the players don't take advantage of the 'hold' it is not your fault; you should not go back on your decision.

....

A number of people report that it is easier to know when to 'hold the whistle' if the umpire has played hockey. They say you have to be 'in the game' to appreciate and understand the player's expectations. This is not always true – referees from other sports or anyone who has a feel for the game (some might call it the X factor), can usually apply advantage very well indeed. Any umpire who reads and understands the game will normally apply some super advantages, irrespective of whether they previously played the game.

• There is rarely an advantage **for** the defence! Their best advantage is you blowing the whistle.

• You should never apply advantage when there is a risk of danger. Try to anticipate the danger and blow the whistle quickly.

• Defending players in possession of the ball in the circle **do not want** advantage. The whistle is always the better option.

• As a beginner, be patient. Don't expect too much too soon. As you gain experience, so you will find yourself applying more advantage, and don't forget to signal it.... there is nothing worse than successfully contributing to the positive flow of the match, only for your colleague (the other umpire) blow the whistle and spoil it all!

• Always discuss advantage with your colleague in your pre-match chat. If you don't do this, there is a virtual guarantee that you will seriously regret it during or after the match. Save yourself and the players the grief! It is very definitely worth it.

Chapter 12

OFFENCES THAT CAN CAUSE CONFUSION

Kicking the ball

Note that the offence is to **kick** the ball. It is not an offence if the ball hits the foot or body of a player unless that player:

- was positioned with the clear intention of stopping the ball or,
- made no effort to avoid being hit by the ball or,
- moved into the path of the ball.

Stopping the ball with the hand or catching the ball

Only the goalkeeper can stop the ball with the hand and only the goalkeeper can catch the ball, but note, he can catch it **only** during a penalty stroke. However, field players must always be entitled to **protect themselves** from the ball and occasionally they will use their hands to do just that. Umpires, you must not penalise them when this happens. What you should do is penalise the player who caused them to protect themselves. **Dangerous play** was the first offence and that's the one for you to penalise.

Playing the ball with the rounded side of the stick

If the ball hits the back of the stick there is no offence. You should consider the same principles as applied for the ball hitting the foot.

- Very often inexperienced players and spectators expect the umpire to blow the whistle **every** time the ball hits a foot or hits the back of a stick. Refrain umpire...encourage the players to play on – where it is safe. There is often an advantage to be had. Signal the advantage, and use your voice to help the players get the message.

Saying "play it" or "play on" is always well received.

- In the Hockey Rules book of 2004 it will specify that a penalty should be awarded only when a player or team has been disadvantaged by an opponent breaking the Rules. If awarding a penalty is not an advantage to the team which did not break the Rules, play must continue. That's a pretty strong message and it really makes sense doesn't it!

Chapter 13

THE MANUFACTURED FOUL AND OTHER OFFENCES

It is often difficult, (especially for those of us who are less experienced), to recognise the manufactured foul. Unfortunately we are witnessing an increase in this area of the game and we need to penalise it more consistently and with more regularity. Until we umpires address these situations, we should not expect the tactics of the players to change.

Every umpire can positively contribute towards the maintenance of fair play – the spirit of the game. The manufactured foul is not permitted and it must be penalised.

To take an example...

An attacking player dribbling the ball towards an opponent in the attacking 23m area. His visible sole intention is to put the ball on the opponents foot. Try and visualise the situation now. You are absolutely certain (and you must be) that the player in possession of the ball is intent on putting it on the opponents foot. You see him recognise but ignore all other options (perhaps there was a pass available to him, he saw it, he ignored it, perhaps he could have turned and carried the ball in another direction, he didn't) – instead he virtually chased the player and put the ball on his foot. What do you do umpire?

Interestingly there could be a variety of answers to this question! It's what many of us call that 'horrible grey area' However, if we are as honest and as brave as a good umpire should be, on condition that we are 100% confident of our assessment of the situation being an accurate

one, we should blow the whistle and award the free-hit to the defender
(to the person who had the ball put on his foot!)

....

• It needs experience to recognise the manufactured
foul and it needs courage to penalise it. If you see it
and you are **absolutely sure** about it...be brave, be
consistent and the players will respect your decision.

....

Other Offences

• Players are not permitted to take part in, or interfere with, the game
unless they are holding their stick. If a player drops their stick, they
are not permitted to chase the play or the ball...unless attempting to
make the umpire smile and then they should be forgiven and thanked!
• It is also an offence to throw or propel the stick at the ball, at a
player, or indeed at anyone.
• Players are not permitted to raise their sticks in a dangerous or
intimidating way and neither are they permitted to dangerously lift
their sticks over the head of an opponent.

....

• The latter is often evident in obstruction situations
and regrettably on occasions, it's left unchallenged by
the umpire. You should penalise this offence. Award the
free-hit if obstruction occurs, but in turn, you should not
permit the player who was obstructed to use their stick
dangerously or illegally.

THE MANUFACTURED FOUL AND OTHER OFFENCES

If you penalise the offence the first time it happens (initially, usually a verbal warning), the players will probably understand - reacting positively, and refraining from repeating it.

• Remember safety must always be your primary consideration for all of the players and you must ensure that every effort is made to secure a safe environment.

....

- Players are not permitted to hit, hook, hold, or strike at another player's stick. Umpires should penalise these offences strictly... especially if they are deliberate.
- Players are not permitted to time-waste. It is often difficult when starting out in umpiring, to recognise time wasting.

....

• You cannot penalise players for time-wasting when the ball is in play! Try to "get inside the player's head". Time wasting offences are usually exclusive to the team who have the upper hand. Perhaps they are 1-0 up with one minute to play. They are hardly going to rush any free-hit you award them. Be aware of this, and if you are confident that they are wasting time, blow you whistle again and award the free-hit the other way – to the opposition.

....

Chapter 14

MISCONDUCT

Misconduct is rough or dangerous play. It is also any delay which amounts to time-wasting, any intentional offence or any bad behaviour. In hockey, intentional offences and misconduct are covered by the same Rule.

On occasions, a minority of players intentionally break the Rules in order to gain an advantage for themselves or their team. An obvious example could be the player who knocks the ball away following the award of a free-hit to the opposition.

Umpires must penalise intentional offences and misconduct promptly and appropriately.

....

- Awarding appropriate penalties for these offences early in the match (the very first time it happens) will usually result in non-repetition of the offence.

- If a player or players demonstrate dissent, the umpire should penalise them straight away. If players dissent at a penalty awarded for them, the umpire can and should reverse the decision. Remember this penalty can only be applied if the first penalty has not been taken (ie the ball has not been played). If you react promptly and effectively, the free-hit should be immediately turned around and awarded to the other team. This application of the Rule really does bring results and subsequently, it's very effective.

If players demonstrate dissent at a penalty awarded against them (far more common needless to say), it is recommended that the umpire advance the free-hit a further 10m up the pitch, or alternatively up-grade the decision. This is also very effective, but can only be applied if the initial penalty has not been taken ie. the ball has not been played. It should be noted that the Rule reads "**up to** 10m" and if the team progress it only 3 or 4m, it's their choice. They don't have to use the full 10m.

!

- You cannot advance a free-hit into the circle. Therefore if the misconduct is from the defending team and the ball is in the 23m area, the up-grade shall apply (ie a penalty corner should be awarded).

- You cannot up-grade from a penalty corner to a penalty stroke. Personal penalties are best in this situation, (ie a warning card and/or a temporary suspension).

- When you reverse a decision following misconduct, you should blow the whistle again and indicate the new penalty and the player/s causing the new decision.

....

It is essential that you give the players time and opportunity to see that you have reversed a decision. They must be allowed to re-position themselves otherwise you in your effort to umpire effectively and as per the Rules of the game, have caused confusion and potential disaster.

From January 2004, in an effort to improve control of player conduct and therefore to protect the image of hockey, the intended duration of a temporary suspension may be extended for misconduct by a player while suspended.

....

- This change will be a positive addition to the penalties available to umpires on condition it is used wisely!

....

Chapter 15

SUBSTITUTION

Captains are responsible for the substitution of their players. Although an increasing number of teams now have managers and coaches, the captain remains primarily responsible.

Before the match starts, confirm with the captains which side of the pitch the substitutions are to take place. All substitutions should be at, or close to, the centre-line from one side of the pitch only. If there are team benches, the substitutions take place from that side of the pitch.

....

- If there's a limited area around the pitch, ask the captains to make sure that the benches are positioned well back from the side-line.

....

Each team is permitted to use up to 5 substitutes and they can enter and re-enter the pitch at any time **except immediately following the award and before the completion of a penalty corner.**

There is no stoppage in play for substitutions, except for goalkeepers. 'Time' is stopped when a goalkeeper is substituted.

Substitutes are not permitted to enter the pitch until the player they are replacing has left it and neither are they permitted as replacements for suspended players.

- Remember that there must always be a goalkeeper on the pitch for each team and if a goalkeeper is suspended, a substitute goalkeeper must enter the pitch, but only on condition that a field player leaves the pitch. If the team doesn't have a second goalkeeper, a field player must take on the role of the goalkeeper and they must be given adequate time to put on protective headgear, a different coloured shirt and other protective equipment if they choose.

- Don't forget...the goalkeeper helmet and a shirt of a different colour are compulsory. They are not optional. Be on hand to offer guidance rather than having to delay the game unnecessarily because the players didn't realise and you didn't help them.

- Don't panic or worry over substitutions. As long as captains are aware that the incoming player does not enter the pitch before the out-going player has left it, you should have very little to oversee.

Chapter 16

POSITIONING

Good positioning is key to good performance. It is considered by the majority to be the most important element of the umpire's game. You can know every Rule in the Rule book and you can have perfect eye-sight, but if you are not in the right place at the right time, the chances of making the required correct decision are measurably reduced.

Hockey is a fast game and with ever improving surfaces and skills, it is getting faster. Umpires must be able and prepared to move throughout the match and sometimes they need to move at speed.

Indeed, it is because of the fast pace of the game that we have two umpires on the pitch. You begin the match on separate and opposite sides of the centre line but as the game commences, you move according to the demands of play, up and down and in and out of the pitch.

You should work as a **team** and recognise that throughout the match you both have a role in the decision-making process. The days of the involved umpire and the non-involved umpire are over and while each umpire remains responsible for blowing the whistle in their own circle, staying in and being solely responsible for decisions 'in your own half' is a principle that is long forgotten.

....

- We now talk about 'the controlling umpire' and the 'assisting umpire' and throughout the game, we adopt one of those two roles...never are we able to rest...to take a mental break.

- Umpires need to think about the benefits of moving deeper into the pitch and further up the pitch. This kind of positioning provides them with better vision, facilitates better rapport with the players, leads to better under-standing on the part of the umpire and of the players and, essentially it lends more credibility to decisions.

- You and your colleague must do your best to control the match well and in order to succeed you need to be close enough to make the right decisions, to see the ball and the play. It's not always easy and it does require a practised ability to read the play and a good level of fitness, but it'll bring much better results than simply 'parking up on the side-lines' or staying on your own defending 23m line...that's really asking for trouble!

- Umpires have historically been advised to try and stay ahead of the play - to keep play on their left. This recommendation remains valid but it is inevitable that on occasions, you are going to be taken by surprise and the ball races up the pitch faster than you can travel! Try not to worry when this happens, move quickly but recognise that it can be easy to recognise an offence from behind the ball – isn't that why so many goalkeepers become umpires when they stop playing?

- The key to good positioning is the ability to read the game, and the better you read it, the easier it will be to stay ahead of it. And if you miss something, don't panic. Your colleague will be close by and watching carefully. Make eye contact and receive and take that assisting signal.

- Imagine that you are on the pitch now. If you stand with your back towards the back-line, you see everything directly in front of you...yes? If you stand with your back towards the side-line, you see everything directly in front of you...yes? Now change the angle of your feet. Position yourself so that the corner flag behind you is directly in line with the middle of your back. You are now standing at an angle and you have a much wider arc of vision. It is this arc that you need to adopt as often as possible.

....

Set-Piece Positioning

Penalty Corner

We have already referred to the relevance of positioning yourself towards the middle of the circle, with one arm held high while encouraging the players to position themselves for a penalty corner. Now consider the 'arc'. Look to see where the players who are likely to be involved are positioned, move yourself into a spot where you are out of their way while adopting a position that provides you with the necessary maximum arc of vision.

Your chosen position should be steered according to the position of the players and their probable path (route) towards the goal. It is possible that you'll start off inside the circle and quite close to the back-line (within a couple of metres of it – particularly if the PC is being taken on the near side). Although far less likely, it is also possible that you take up a position more towards the circle edge. The key is that wherever you start you must be prepared to move, you must be and stay out of the way of the players (attack and defence) and the ball and, you must be able to see the ball at all times. Not much to ask is it!

....

- There are some occasions when being close to the near post in a PC situation is appropriate and there are others when it is not. Be steered only by the position of the players and the ball (plus essentially your own comfort).

- You will know when you're in a position that allows you to see everything and as you gain more experience, so as it gets easier. If you are caught in a position that leaves you unable to see the ball / play, look to your colleague who should be there to immediately offer you that crucial assisting signal.

....

For penalty corners on the far-side of your circle, you are likely to be anywhere between 5m into the circle from the back-line, and a couple of metres off your near post. (Refer to the diagram). Try it and see what's best for you but remember that it will always be governed by your confidence, your ability to read the game, your level of mobility and the skill level and position of the players and the ball.

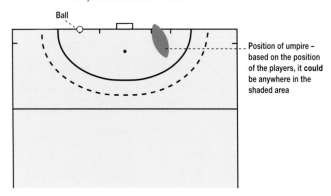

Penalty corner from the far-side

Ball

Position of umpire – based on the position of the players, it **could** be anywhere in the shaded area

So where is your colleague while all of this is going on? He should be approximately 8-10m into the pitch (from the side-line) and 8-10m into your half (from the centre line) and, essentially, he should be watching carefully. You may need his assistance if you lose sight of the ball at any stage or if you see an off the ball incident but aren't positive as to how or who started it! A good example of needing your colleague to be attentive is when the ball is around your far post area. Was the ball going into the goal or wasn't it? Where was the player's foot when the ball struck it?

If your colleague is appropriately positioned he should be able to give you the assisting signal immediately you look to him.

- Next time you watch a match that has experienced umpires officiating, look at them carefully during penalty

corner situations and see how they work together as a team. See how they communicate their readiness and control and see how they position themselves.

....

Penalty corner from the near-side

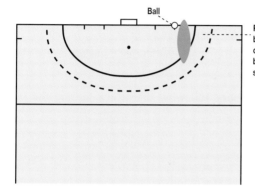

Ball

Position of umpire – based on the position of the players, it **could** be anywhere in the shaded area

Penalty Stroke

Many people are surprised to learn that both umpires are involved in the penalty stroke. The umpire who awarded the stroke (the controlling umpire) should position himself in the circle approximately 3m behind and to the right of the taker, and the other umpire (the assisting umpire) should position himself on or near the back-line approximately 5 to 7m from the far goal-post (that is the far post in the eyes of the umpire controlling the stroke).

The role of the umpire who awarded the stroke is to control the penalty stroke. He needs to be able to clearly see both the taker and the goalkeeper.

The role of the other umpire is only to see that the ball wholly crosses the goal-line, or not as the case may be! Again the umpires act as a team.

Centre Pass

Each umpire should be midway between their 23m line and the centre line and approximately 10m from the side-line into the pitch.

Hit-In from the side-line

It is recommended that umpires keep play on their left during a hit-in. Don't allow yourself to be too distant and always be aware of the importance of credibility. The players need to know that you can see the ball and the play, allowing you to make the correct decision.

Hit-Out (taken by the defence following the attack putting the ball over the back-line)

This used to be referred to as the '16 yards hit'. It is now known simply as a 'hit-out' and in terms of umpire positioning, the best place is always determined by the position of the players, never too far away and ideally not square. Most umpires prefer to be out wide and a little behind the level of the ball.

- Always be aware of the possibility of this hit being intercepted by a fast and skilful attacker. Be on your guard.

Corner

Corners are taken on the side-line, 5m from the corner of the pitch.

All opposition players are to be a minimum of 5m from the ball until it is played. The players have more options now that corners are taken here and we umpires need to be aware of all the possibilities of play. We need to see the players across the pitch and in and around the circle, plus the

23m area and, of course, the taker. Again the 'arc' is very important.

For corners on the near-side, it is probably best to position yourself either to the right of the taker towards the corner, or behind the back-line on the edge of the pitch, or (pending the position of the players), slightly to the left of the taker looking in on an arc facing the goal. As always, it is determined by the position of the players and your own level of experience. The more games you umpire, the better you will be able to read the potential of play and decide on the best spot. Once the corner is taken, move according to the demands of play. Do not stand still.

For corners on the far-side of the pitch, the preferred view is between the near post and the centre of the circle towards the back-line... but be very careful and very alert. Be ready to move quickly for although it's a great place to see from, you are likely to be in the way of the players, particularly the goalkeeper – something to be avoided at all times!

....

- For corners taken on the far side of the pitch, rely on your colleague to penalise the lifted ball...should it occur. He should be positioned within a few metres of your 23m line. Incidentally, this is another key area to discuss in your pre-match chat.

....

Hit-Out

....

- Never assume that the players don't make silly errors. Try to position yourself so as you are ready to cope with anything.

....

Bully

Position yourself close to the bully – 5 to 10m is usually a good place to be, but if that isn't practical, then simply be as close as is sensible and remember...from January 2004, sticks will be required to touch only once.

Free-Hit

You will need to use your experience and know your ability to read the game. Do not take unnecessary risks. When the free hit is in the middle of the pitch, you will need to think about keeping play reasonably on your left and be far enough into the pitch to maintain and assert control.

When the free hit is deep in your colleague's half of the pitch, you will need to remain focused...stay with it! Don't be unnecessarily distant and avoid being distracted.

Open Play

When the ball is in open play in your half of the pitch, try to position yourself approximately 15 to 20m from play. Sometimes you can afford to be closer. In the other half of the pitch, your positioning will be steered according to (1) your level of experience and ability to read the game, (2) your speed and mobility and (3) common sense.

....

- Don't distance yourself to the degree that you become lost. It won't help you or your colleague and it certainly won't help the game.

....

Chapter 17

SUSPENSION OF PLAYERS

There is a very sensible warning procedure practised in hockey. Umpires carry a set of colour coded warning cards and if used appropriately they are really effective. The cards are coloured green, yellow and red and they are usually awarded in that order!

The green card represents a warning, the yellow a temporary suspension and the red, a permanent suspension and complete removal from the playing area.

Players can be suspended for a number of reasons and for varying lengths of time. The minimum suspension time in outdoor hockey is 5 minutes.

....

- The key is to know how to you use the cards well. The yellow card is serious business for the players. They don't want to be sent out of the game. You must always be positive that your decision is the right one when awarding a yellow.

- The minimum suspension of 5 minutes is usually representative of an intentional technical offence or unintentional but repeated technical offences. Physical offences are usually punished with a 10 minute suspension and players and coaches increasingly understand and expect this type of consistency.

- Umpires should not substitute any red card offence for a very lengthy yellow card. If a red card is deserved, it must shown – for the benefit of the players, the game and the sport. Don't be tempted to think that a 40 minutes temporary suspension is an acceptable alternative for any red card offence.

So where does a temporarily suspended player go and how do you judge how long the suspension should be? Historically the umpires have sent the offending player off the pitch and directed them to stand behind their own goal. In today's hockey, it is preferred to send the offending player to the team bench (assuming that there is such a thing) or even better to a "sin-bin" chair placed next to the team bench. There the player has an opportunity to calm down in a more comfortable environment and they feel less alienated and are better able to prepare for their return to the pitch.

- What if the suspended player doesn't manage to remain calm or he throws his stick or shouts and curses while sitting in the sin-bin? A really effective

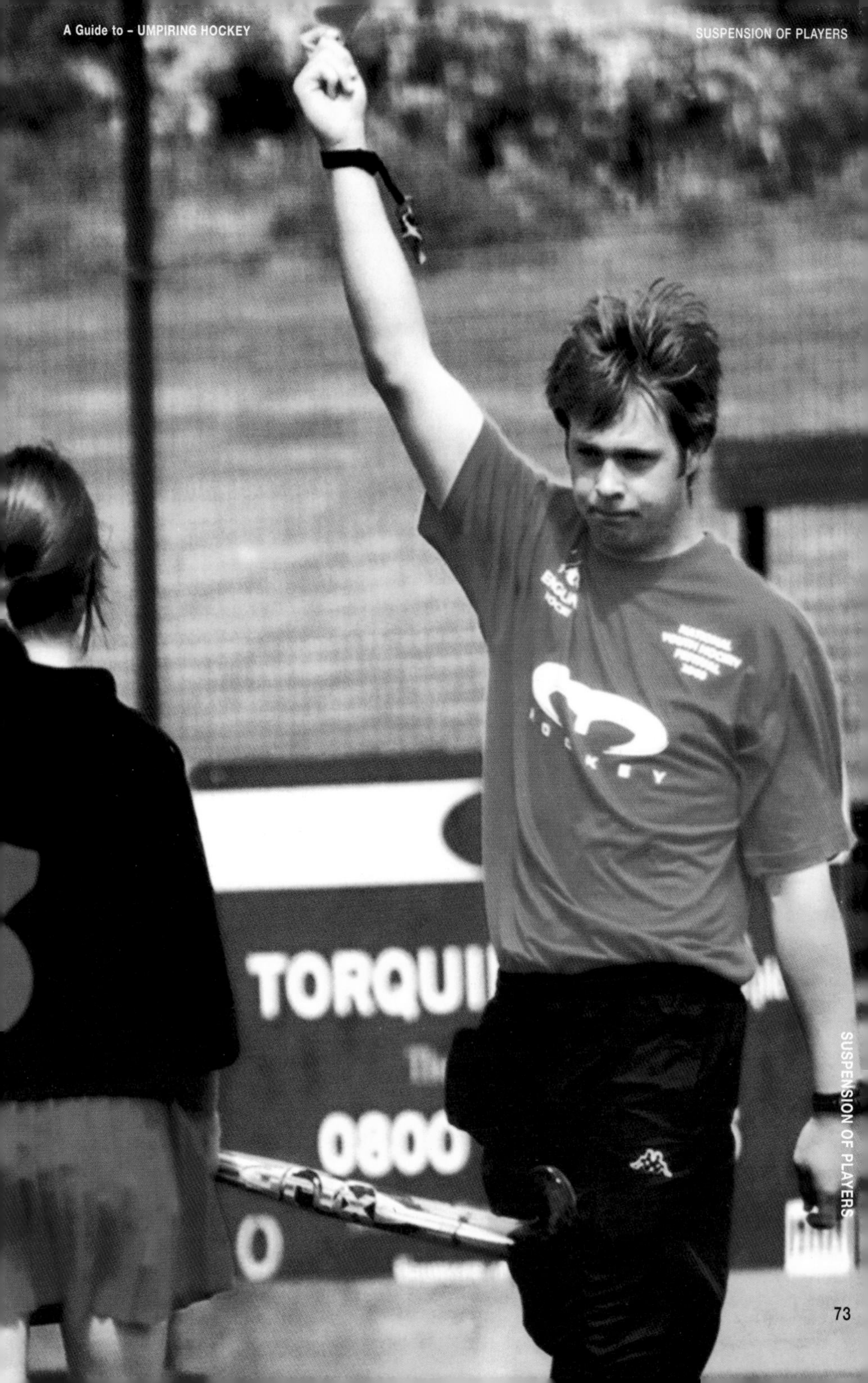
TORQUI
0800

option is to stop the game and the time and call the team captain. Get him involved in the situation, ask him to sort out the problem before you are forced to take further action. However, from January 2004 there is a change to the Rule. The umpire could still opt to get the captain involved and ask him to calm the player but the new alternative will be to lengthen the suspension time (ie instead of the original 5 minutes suspension, it becomes 10 minutes). The umpire should advise the suspended player and the team captain.

In tournament hockey, there is usually a Technical Table with a Tournament Officer or Delegate and they supervise the suspended player/s in a seating area close to the technical table.

• A player can be given two green cards in one game if he commits two separate and different offences. The same can apply with a yellow card - if the offences are separate and different in type, the offending player can receive a second yellow. However, it is usually a more lengthy suspension than the first. Of course there are occasions when this would be wholly inappropriate, and the red card is the best option.

• It is essential that the umpire is sensible when awarding a red card.

Once it's shown, the options start to reduce.
In other words, if you can do it to one player, if another commits the same offence you are obliged to apply the same penalty.

• When you award a warning card of any colour, try not to be confrontational. In the majority of cases the player will be frustrated or angry; he may be particularly cross with himself or perhaps you. Do not react aggressively towards him.

• Always try to be calm when showing a card.
Beckon the player towards you with an open palm as opposed to an aggressive point and, walk part of the way towards him (30% of the distance is "the common norm."). When you are satisfied that the player has acknowledged that it is him that you are calling (signalling) in your direction and he has walked towards you, hold the appropriate warning card high in the air so as your colleague, the offending player and the other players can see it clearly. If the card is yellow, you should immediately direct him towards the designated suspension area. Try to avoid making any verbal comments, threats or accusations, but if you are asked "What was it for?", or "What have I done?", reply briefly and positively.

• Silence on the part of the umpire is not recommended when the player asks a question. If you choose to ignore the question, you will probably cause the player to become frustrated and the situation could worsen.

• Always use your common sense when showing warning cards. Sometimes the player is calm and sometimes he isn't. Usually he will be frustrated at the very least. You must manage the situation with control and confidence and never touch the player if he appears angry or aggressive.

Chapter 18

ACCIDENTS AND INJURIES

As an umpire, one of your most important responsibilities is the provision of a safe environment for all of the players. Obviously every match has an unavoidable degree of risk for the participants, but the umpire's control and application of fair play within the Rules of the game should contribute strongly to a safe match.

But what if there is an incident or an injury? What should happen and who should control and manage it? The answer is you should!

If a player receives a minor injury, he should leave the pitch and be replaced by a substitute and it shouldn't be necessary for you to blow the whistle or stop the time. If the injury is more serious and he can't leave the pitch (perhaps he has been hit on the knee by a fast ball) you should blow the whistle and you should stop the time. Immediately you do this, move quickly towards the player and assess as to whether he can be moved / needs treatment. Obviously if the team has a physiotherapist you can then call him on to the pitch. If the team doesn't have a physio (and for most club hockey this is the case) you are advised to leave the decision regarding moving the player and/or treating the player exclusively to the captain and the team. Do not insist that the player be moved and do not offer treatment yourself unless you are qualified to give it.

There are occasions, when a player is seriously injured and prompt action is required. A good example is if someone receives a head injury. You should blow the whistle and stop time immediately. There should be no hesitation.

- If a player injures himself and is bleeding, the Rules require him to leave the pitch at the first opportunity and have the wound cleaned and dressed. It is worth noting that there are occasions when players do not realise they have sustained an injury of this nature. Do not get over excited umpires! At the first opportunity, calmly ask the player to leave the pitch and get attention. You can often do this without blowing the whistle and interrupting the game.

- Treatment on the pitch is not permitted in high level games (international hockey or major tournaments and national events) but in club hockey it is common. Always do your best to allow players time to recover and be sympathetic and cooperative. Ask them if they are OK or if they want to leave the pitch. Actions such as these will enhance your rapport with the players and often, surprisingly, lead to approving discussion after the game.

Protecting yourself

It would be foolish to end this book of guidance without mentioning the importance of being suitably **insured**. Sport is witnessing an increasing risk of litigation involving people in officiating roles. This is not something specific to hockey. It happens in rugby, football, cricket, and many other sports. Make sure that you have adequate insurance cover, (public liability), to protect and address any such risk. If you need further information on insurance, check your club policy or contact your local umpiring association or administrator and establish exactly what cover you have or what is available to you.

And finally and most importantly, enjoy your umpiring. Smile when it's appropriate to do so, talk when it's appropriate to do so, apologise when it's appropriate to do so. Your's is a very important role - take it seriously and do your best in every game.